HAPPY THANKSGIVING
Jokes
and
Riddles

for Kids Ages 8-12

Edited by Emily McKeon

This Book Belongs to:

_____

_____

THANKS!

Thank you for your purchase. If you enjoyed this book, please consider dropping us a review by scanning the QR code. It takes only 5 seconds and helps small independent publishers like ours.

Scripto Love
PRESS

HAPPY THANKSGIVING JOKES AND RIDDLES FOR KIDS

Spot illustrations: Creative Fabrica & Freepik.com

Contents

Introduction

Add a little joy this Thanksgiving Day with Happy *Thanksgiving Jokes and Riddles for Kids*! Jam-packed with festive jokes, riddles, and puns about all things Thanksgiving, it's sure to stuff your holiday with laughter.

Whether you're reading alone, or with family and friends, you'll gobble up the laughs with this festive joke book!

1

Gobble 'Til You Wobble

What do sweet potatoes wear to bed?

Yammies!

What did the Thanksgiving turkey say to the Christmas ham?

"Nice to meat you!"

Why don't side dishes tell jokes?

They're too corny!

What do you call a sad cranberry?

A blueberry!

What do you need to make Thanksgiving s'mores?

Pil-grahms!

Do you know where you can get turkey stock in bulk?

Stock market!

What do you tell your jokester cousin on Thanksgiving?

"You're on a casse-roll!"

What does grandma say when you burn the holiday meal?

"Oh, good gravy!"

Why did the cranberries turn red?

Because they saw the turkey dressing!

Knock, knock!

Who's there?

Feather.

Feather who?

Feather last time, please pass the dinner rolls!

Why should you never set the turkey next to the dessert?

Because he will gobble, gobble it up!

What is a turkey's favorite dessert?

Peach gobbler!

Why was the Thanksgiving soup so expensive?

It had 24 carrots!

What role do green beans play in Thanksgiving dinner?

The casse-role!

How did the salt and pepper welcome all the guests?

By saying, "Seasoning's greetings!"

What vegetables would you like with your Thanksgiving dinner?

Beets me!

Why did the policeman stop you on your way home last Thanksgiving?

Because you far exceeded your feed limit!

"How'd the Thanksgiving cheese plate go over?"

"Everyone was grateful!"

"How was the butternut squash soup?"

"It was gourd!"

Knock knock!

Who's there?

Harry.

Harry who?

Harry up, it's almost Thanksgiving!

"I tried a new pie recipe."

"Wow, you're a real
pie-oneer!"

**What's Frankenstein's
favorite
Thanksgiving dish?**

Monster mash potatoes
and grave-y!

**What can never ever
be eaten for
Thanksgiving dinner?**

Thanksgiving breakfast!

What Thanksgiving side dish could be given out at Halloween?

Candied yams!

Why did the apple pie go to the dentist?

Because it needed a filling!

What do you call a small pepper in late autumn?

A little chili!

Knock knock!

Who's there?

Don.

Don who?

Don eat all the gravy, I want some more!

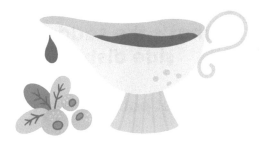

What can a whole apple do that half an apple can't do?

It can look round!

What's the best thing to put into a pumpkin pie?

Your teeth!

What's the saddest side dish?

Sweet potato cries!

What did the apple say to the pie baker?

"Use cherries instead!"

What's an elephant's favorite vegetable?

Squash!

Why did the apple pie cry?

Its peelings were hurt!

Knock, knock!

Who's there?

Butter.

Butter who?

Butter open up quick, I have a funny Thanksgiving joke to tell you!

What do you get when you cross a train engine with an apple pie?

Puff pastry!

Which Thanksgiving beverage is sad?

Apple sigh-der!

What kind of nuts always seems to have a cold?

Cashews!

2

The Baste Turkey Jokes

Why do turkeys hate the kitchen on Thanksgiving?

It smells fowl!

What do you call gossiping with a turkey at the table?

A side dish!

Who didn't have any friends at Friendsgiving?

The turkey!

What does the turkey think about holidays?

They're about family time, after that, it's all gravy!

Why are turkeys good at rebelling?

They love a coup!

Why did the turkey run across the road?

It was time for dinner!

Knock knock!

Who's there?

Tamara.

Tamara who?

Tamara we'll eat all the leftovers!

What key won't open a door?

A tur-key!

What sound does a limping turkey make?

Wobble, wobble!

What do turkeys do on Sunday?

Have a peck-nics!

Why didn't the turkey want dessert?

He was stuffed!

Why do turkeys hate Thanksgiving tables?

They're a fowl sight!

What do you call a turkey the day after Thanksgiving?

Lucky!

Knock, knock!

Who's there?

Dishes!

Dishes who?

Dishes the best Thanksgiving ever!

What sound does a turkey's phone make?

Wing wing wing!

What was the turkey thankful for on Thanksgiving?

Vegetarians!

Can a turkey jump higher than a house?

Yes, because houses can't jump!

Why do turkeys love rainy days?

They love fowl weather!

Why do turkeys gobble?

Because they never learned table manners!

What's a popular Thanksgiving dance?

The turkey trot!

Why do turkeys only star in R-rated movies?

Because they use fowl language!

When do you serve rubber turkey?

Pranksgiving!

What do you call a running turkey?

Fast food!

Knock knock!

Who's there?

Phillip.

Phillip who?

Phillip your plate and dig in!

Why did the turkey play the drums in his band?

Because he already had drumsticks!

What did the turkey say to the computer?

"Google, google!"

Who is not hungry at Thanksgiving?

The turkey, because he's already stuffed!

**If you call a large turkey
a gobbler, what do you
call a small one?**

A goblet!

**What did the turkey say
to the turkey hunter on
Thanksgiving Day?**

"Quack, quack!"

**Why was the turkey
arrested?**

The police suspected
fowl play!

Knock, knock!

Who's there?

Olive.

Olive who?

Olive you!

Why shouldn't you sit next to a turkey at dinner?

Because he will gobble it up!

What type of glass does a turkey drink from?

A goblet!

What happened to the turkey that got in a fight?

He got the stuffing knocked out of him!

Knock knock!

Who's there?

Possum.

Possum who?

Possum gravy on my mashed potatoes!

Why did the turkey cross the road?

Because it was the chicken's day off!

What did Han Solo say to Luke Skywalker on Thanksgiving?

"May the forks be with you!"

What was the turkey's favorite pop song?

All About That Baste!

3

Puckish Pilgrims

What do you call an attractive pilgrim?

A puri-ten!

What did the Pilgrim wear to dinner?

A har-vest!

What kind of music did the Pilgrims like?

Plymouth Rock!

If April showers bring
May flowers, what do
May flowers bring?

Pilgrims!

What kind of tan did
pilgrims get at the beach?

Puri-tan!

What do you call the
age of a pilgrim?

Pilgrimage!

What did pilgrims use to bake cookies?

May-flour!

Why didn't the pilgrim want to make the bread?

It's a crummy job!

What's the smallest unit of measurement in the pilgrim cookbook?

Pil-gram!

What kind of face does a pilgrim make when he's in pain?

Pil-grimace!

Why do Pilgrims' pants always fall down?

Because they wear their buckles on their hats!

If the Pilgrims were still alive, what would they be most famous for?

Their age!

Knock, knock!

Who's there?

Annie.

Annie who?

Annie body seen the turkey?

4

Unbe-leaf-able Autumn Jokes

What is the best book to read in autumn?

Gourd of the Rings!

Why was the man shopping for Reynolds Wrap?

His wife wanted to see
fall foilage!

How did the tree get a new job?

She had the right
qua-leaf-ications!

Why was the robot couple's anniversary in the fall?

They were autumn mated!

What do Jedi trees say to each other in the fall?

"May the forest be with you!"

What do farmers wear under their shirt when they're cold?

A har-vest!

How do trees get on the Internet?

They just log on!

Why shouldn't you tell a secret in a cornfield?

Because the corn has ears!

How do you fix a broken pumpkin?

With a pumpkin patch!

Knock Knock!

Who's there?

Arthur.

Arthur who?

Arthur any drumsticks left?

What happened when the turkey got in a fight?

The stuffing was
knocked out of him!

What is it called when a tree takes some time off?

Paid leaf!

Why does Humpty Dumpty love autumn so much?

Because he had a great fall!

Why did the pumpkin lose the boxing match?

He let his gourd down!

What do lumberjacks shout at the start of fall?

"Sep-timberrrrrr!"

Why do trees hate going to school in the fall?

Because they're easily stumped!

Knock, knock!

Who's there?

Holly.

Holly who?

Holly days like Thanksgiving are wonderful!

What's the best band to listen to in autumn?

The Spice Girls!

What did the leaf say to the other leaf?

"I'm falling for you!"

Why do birds fly south for the fall?

Because it's quicker than walking!

Knock, knock!

Who's there?

Handsome.

Handsome who?

Handsome cranberry dressing to me, please!

Why are trees so carefree and easy going?

Because every fall, they let loose!

Why did the scarecrow win a Nobel Prize?

He was outstanding in his field!

What do the leaves say before they hibernate?

"Rake me up when September ends!"

What happens when winter arrives?

Autumn leaves!

Why did the Jack-o'-lantern look after the pie?

They were pump-kin!

What is it called when a tree doesn't think it's autumn?

Disbe-leaf!

Why's it so easy to trick a leaf in October?

They fall for anything!

Why is autumn the proudest season?

It's fall of it!

What do short-sighted ghouls wear?

Spooktacles!

**Why are apples so bad
in interrogations?**

They always crumble!

**How do leaves get from
place to place?**

Autumn-mobiles!

**What is worse than finding
a worm in your apple?**

Finding half of a worm!

Knock, knock!

Who's there?

Don.

Don who?

Don eat all the pumpkin pie!

What is the cutest season?

Aww-tumn!

What's the ratio of a pumpkin's circumference to its diameter?

Pumpkin Pi!

How are you supposed to talk in the apple library?

With your in-cider voice!

Who lives in the scary Hundred Acre Wood?

Winnie the Boo!

Who helps the little pumpkins cross the road when they go to school?

The traffic gourd!

Who won the skeleton beauty contest?

No body!

What is a scarecrow's favorite fruit?

Straw-berries!

What room are ghosts not allowed to enter?

The living room!

What's a fire's least favorite month?

No-ember!

What did the ground say when fall came?

"Well that's a re-leaf!"

Which sport is the pumpkin's favorite?

Squash!

What do you call a fat pumpkin?

A plumpkin!

Why did the apple stop in the middle of the road?

Because it ran out of juice!

How do gourds get so strong?

By pumpkin iron!

Why do pumpkins sit on people's porches?

They don't have any hands to knock on the door!

Knock knock!

Who's there?

May.

May who?

Mayflowers bloom by Plymouth rock!

What did the farmer say when his gourds went missing?

"There's pumpkin strange going on around here!"

How did the pilgrim quit smoking tobacco?

Cold turkey!

What kind of coat goes on wet?

A coat of paint!

**What can you see in fall
that you can't see in
spring, summer, or winter?**

The word "all!"

**What kind of an apple isn't
an apple?**

A pineapple!

**When does Christmas come
before Thanksgiving?**

When you're looking at
a dictionary!

5
Gridiron Grins

What's a football player's favorite ice cream?

Any given sundae!

What did the football coach say to the broken candy machine?

"Give me my quarterback!"

Where did the goblin throw the football at recess?

Over the ghoul line!

What is it called when a dinosaur gets a touchdown?

A dino-score!

Where do football players dance?

At a foot ball!

Why didn't the skeleton play football?

His heart wasn't in it!

What did the football player say to the flight attendant?

"Put me in coach!"

Why can't you play football with pigs?

They hog the ball!

Why is it always warmer after a football game?

All the fans have left!

How did Scrooge end up with the football?

The ghost of Christmas passed!

Where do hungry football players play?

In the Supper Bowl!

Who are the happiest people at the football game?

The cheerleaders!

Why was Cinderella so bad at football?

Her coach was a pumpkin!

When is a football player like a judge?

When he sits on the bench!

Which insect loves football the most?

The fumble bee!

6

Clever Autumn Riddles

The annual tradition each and every Thanksgiving Day is watching the great team sport the Lions and Cowboys play. What is it?

ANSWER: A football game.

It has ears but it cannot hear and it has flakes but it has no hair. What is it?

ANSWER: Corn.

What smells the best every Thanksgiving dinner?

ANSWER: Your nose.

Most people eat me, and that is no surprise. I taste great as chips and also as fries. What am I?

ANSWER: A potato.

Why didn't the Pilgrims tell each other their secrets in the cornfield?

ANSWER:
Because the corn had ears.

This key has legs, but can't open a door. What is it?

ANSWER: Tur-key.

It's something I spy with my little eye. I'm an orange squash that is baked in a pie. What am I?

ANSWER: A pumpkin.

If you like sweet side dishes, then I will make you a happy fellow as I have sweet potatoes as well as sugar and marshmallow. What am I?

ANSWER: Candied yams.

Which side of the turkey has the most feathers?

ANSWER: The outside.

There's lots of this at Thanks-giving but you don't want it to be wasted because its meat's really juicy, just so long as it has been basted. What is it?

ANSWER: Turkey.

What do the Pilgrims, the Indi-ans, and the Puritans all have in common?

ANSWER: The letter "I."

Is it possible for a turkey to fly higher than an ostrich?

ANSWER:: Yes, ostriches don't fly.

You see this festive event along the street on this very special day, from Felix to Mickey to Dora and Bugs Bunny, all of the people will make way. What is it?

ANSWER: The Thanksgiving Day Parade.

It's eaten at Thanksgiving as part of the main course. It gets added to your plate in the form of a sauce. What is it?

ANSWER: Cranberry.

What's blue and covered with lots of feathers?

ANSWER: A turkey holding its breath.

If you want to picture fall, then my image would be best. I am a horn that is filled with all the season's harvest. What am I?

ANSWER: Cornucopia.

We sailed from Europe so we'd have the freedom to worship, and overcome many obstacles, we finally reached land at Cape Cod. Who are we?

ANSWER: The Pilgrims.

I'm a berry, but I'm not sweet. What am I?

ANSWER: A cranberry.

7

Fall-ing for Puns

Fall is a-maize-ing.

Pumpkin spice, spice, baby.

Humpty Dumpty had a great fall —hope you do too!

Hay there!

This cooler weather is soup-er.

I yam what I yam.

Don't even chai.

Orange you glad it's fall?

Let's pumpkin spice things
up a bit.

I like you a latte.

Witch fall flavor is your favorite?

Pumpkin spice and everything nice.

You truly a-maize me!

This maze is going to be a piece
of spice cake.

My favorite fall outfit is a har-vest.

Easy as pumpkin pie.

You're the candy apple of my eye.

If you don't love fall,
leaf me alone.